# TORTILLAS

# TORTILLAS

### W. PARK KERR

William Morrow and Company, Inc.

New York

A million thanks to Harriet Bell, editor; Louise Fili, designer; Betty Alfenito, prop stylist; Anne Disrude, food stylist; Ellen Silverman, photographer; Janice Faber and Virginia Mayo, assistants

To John Werner and Carrie Brown con amor

# Introduction

❋

TO SOUTHWESTERN AND MEXICAN COOKS, A MEAL THAT DOESN'T INCLUDE TORTILLAS JUST ISN'T WORTH SERVING AT ALL. If the main course isn't actually made with tortillas (fried tortillas filled with shredded meat to make tacos, baked sauced tortillas as chilaquiles or enchiladas, and so on into tortilla infinity), then a basket full of the piping hot flatbreads is present for sopping up every last spicy mouthful.

Tortillas are much more than a snack food. The Aztecs based much of their culture on the reverence for corn (which they called *toconayo,* "our meat"), believing that the gods created humans from the grain. Although corn has excellent keeping qualities when dried, it gets hard as a rock. To aid softening, dried kernels (chicos) are soaked with the mineral lime and then hulled and ground into a thick dough called masa. The masa is flattened into rounds and cooked on a hot stone. This procedure has remained unchanged for centuries, although many of today's cooks make their tortillas from the readily available powdered corn flour called masa harina and cook them on a griddle. The cooks in northern Mexico often make wheat tortillas, which are more flexible than their corn cousins, and stuff and roll them into the big fat burritos beloved by hearty eaters on both sides of the border.

Nothing beats the flavor of a freshly made corn or flour tortilla hot off the griddle, slathered with butter (at breakfast you are allowed the extra treat of drizzling this prize with honey). When I was growing up in El Paso, tortillas were found everywhere. We bought them from small, family-run tortillerias or sometimes from home cooks who made them in their own kitchens to earn a little extra cash. Some American grocery stores carried them, but the ones smuggled back across the border from the market in Juárez tasted even better—the clandestine transport turned them into "forbidden fruit." Wrapped in foil or butcher paper, the just-made tortillas, like any fresh bread, were to be savored the same day as purchase—freezing leftover tortillas was a last resort.

There are so many ways to use tortillas, I don't have a particular favorite, but there are some typically El Paso ways to treat a tortilla. I am very partial to those Rio Grande specialties, flautas, deep-fried flute-shaped corn tortillas filled with shredded meat and dipped in a pool of sour cream. The thick gravy from El Paso-style chili or stew is so good you want to lick it out of the bowl, but the more refined diners in my neck of the woods know that the sauce tastes better when wiped out of its container with a thick pad of folded flour tortilla. And more than one burger stand in Texas serves "hamburguesas" rolled in flour tortillas (instead of boring old buns) and topped with pickled jalapeños. A tortilla is like a blank canvas waiting to be painted, and creative cooks are constantly coming up with new ways to feature them in dishes. In today's "anything goes as long as it tastes good" culinary atmosphere, you are just as likely to encounter tostadas topped with grilled fish as the overly familiar ground beef, beans, and shredded iceberg.

Tortillas have firmly established themselves in American food culture. At my house my two-year-old loves peanut butter and jelly tortillas, and he may be in college before he learns that grilled cheese sandwiches aren't supposed to be round. I'm surprised more of those popular parenting books don't discuss the importance of teaching your child the finer points of tortilla consumption. Well, this book will be a start, at least.

# Corn-Red Chile Tortillas

**M**ANY SUPERMARKETS IN THE WESTERN STATES CARRY REFRIG-ERATED PLASTIC BAGS OF PREPARED MASA, the dough used to make fresh corn tortillas. Most of us will have to make do with masa harina, a flour made from lime-slaked dried corn. Using Red Chile Purée (page 57) as part of the liquid for the dough gives the tortillas an earthy red color and muted spiciness. A tortilla press (see Mail-Order Sources, page 61) makes the job easier than patting them out by hand, a talent that seems to be inborn, although it can be mastered if practiced long enough—say, three meals a day for five or six years. Take the advice of the inspiring authority on Mexican food, Diana Kennedy, and use plastic bags to keep the moist dough from sticking to the tortilla press.

2 cups masa harina
⅓ cup hot water

1 cup Red Chile Purée (page 57) or
frozen red chile purée, thawed

In a mixing bowl, stir together the masa harina, hot water, and chile purée. Knead until a soft but not runny dough forms. (If it seems dry, sprinkle additional water over the dough and knead it in; if it seems wet, knead in a little extra masa harina.) Divide the dough into 14 equal pieces. Cover with plastic wrap.

Heat a well-seasoned cast-iron griddle or skillet over medium heat. Open the tortilla press. Lay one plastic bag on the plate of the press. Center a ball of dough on the baggie. Lay a second plastic bag over the ball of dough. Close the press and push down to form a 6-inch round. Lay the dough-plastic bag combination on the palm of one hand. Peel the upper plastic bag off the dough. Turn the dough-plastic bag combination over so that the dough is supported by your fingers. Peel the second plastic bag off the dough (don't try to peel the dough off the plastic bag—it won't work).

Slap the tortilla onto the griddle. Bake 15 seconds, then turn and bake 30 seconds. Turn once more and bake another 15 seconds, or until the tortilla is cooked through but still soft and flexible (this is a function of how thick or thin you have made your tortilla). Transfer to a napkin-lined basket if you are serving immediately, or cool on a clean towel, wrap airtight, and store at room temperature until using. Repeat with the remaining balls of dough.

# Oregano-Flecked Flour Tortillas

WHEAT TORTILLAS ARE A SPECIALTY IN SONORA, A STATE IN THE NORTHERN PART OF MEXICO. Because America and Mexico share such a long border, Sonoran cooks acquired a taste for our wheat-based breads (just as southwestern American cooks assimilated corn tortillas into their cooking), and wheat tortillas established a popularity that is not found in the other parts of the country. This basic recipe is similar to Diana Kennedy's, but I like to add minced fresh oregano to the dough to give color and flavor. For plain flour tortillas, simply omit the oregano.

1 pound (about 4 scant cups) bread flour
1/2 cup solid vegetable shortening
2 tablespoons minced fresh oregano (optional)

1 teaspoon salt
About 1 cup warm water

In a mixing bowl, work together the flour and shortening (use fingertips or a table fork). Stir in the oregano. Dissolve the salt in the water. Gradually stir the water into the flour mixture until a moist dough forms. Turn the dough out onto a floured work surface and knead by hand for about 5 minutes, or until the dough is smooth and elastic. Divide the dough into 14 equal balls. Cover the balls with greased plastic wrap and let rest in a warm place for 25 minutes.

Over medium heat, warm a well-seasoned very large cast-iron griddle or skillet. On an unfloured surface, using a rolling pin, roll out a ball of dough to about 6 inches in diameter. Pick up the dough, lay it over the backs of your cupped hands and gently work and stretch it out to about 10 inches in diameter (watch a good pizza maker for the right moves—no need to toss your tortilla in the air, though, unless you want to).

Lay the tortilla on the griddle, wait a few seconds, then turn over and bake for another few seconds. The tortilla should be cooked but still flexible and perhaps attractively scorched in spots. Fold into quarters, then transfer to a napkin-lined basket if you are serving the tortillas immediately, or cool completely on a clean towel, wrap airtight, and store at room temperature until serving. Repeat with the remaining balls of dough.

# Stacking Up Tortillas

●

**L**IKE SAVORING JUST-BAKED BREAD, ENJOYING A FRESHLY PRE-
PARED TORTILLA HOT OFF THE GRIDDLE with a pat of butter is one of
life's great culinary pleasures. After you've had that experience, tortillas from the market
will not stack up to fresh ones. Even though store-bought tortillas may not be as good as
homemade, not all supermarket varieties are unacceptable, although there are plenty of
crummy tortillas on the shelves. You may have to search a little to find a good brand you
like, but it's out there. If you live in a city with a sizable Hispanic population, there may
be a small tortilla factory (tortilleria) near you. The wares are sold on the same day they
are made and are meant to be used on the same day as purchase—don't refrigerate them.

Most cooks will have to depend on refrigerated tortillas from the supermarket. The
slightly homely, less pretty tortillas are often the best. If irregularly shaped, thinner or
thicker in spots, or even a little scorched, the tortillas have probably been partially hand-
made, and that's good. Try to choose a brand that is locally produced. Some brands taste
more like cardboard than corn or wheat, and when you find a brand you like, don't forget
its name. Avoid unrefrigerated tortillas. They are usually loaded with preservatives, and
taste a little weird when reheated (and since all tortillas are best warm, you don't have
much chance of improving them).

Warming tortillas not only makes them tastier but increases their flexibility for rolling.
There are several methods for heating tortillas:

1. Stack up to six tortillas and wrap tightly in aluminum foil. Bake in a preheated
   350°F oven until heated through, about 15 minutes. If you want to serve tortillas
   throughout the meal, prepare a number of stacks and stagger their baking times.
2. Cook tortillas directly on a preheated heavy skillet or griddle over medium heat, cooking for about 10 seconds on each side. (Flour tortillas take slightly longer than corn.)
   They may scorch a little, but that's okay—it adds a smoky flavor. Cook only until
   flexible, not brittle.
3. Bake flour tortillas directly on the oven racks in a preheated 450°F oven until
   flexible, about 30 seconds.
4. Grill flour tortillas about 6 inches from the source of heat on a gas or charcoal grill,
   turning once, until flexible, about 30 seconds.

Kindly put, cold tortillas aren't too tasty, so immediately wrap them in a cloth nap-
kin to keep warm and toasty throughout the meal (if you are serving them like bread to
sop up gravies), or use an electric bun warmer.

You can freeze flour tortillas, but the corn ones don't freeze well. The good news is that dry, slightly stale corn tortillas have plenty of uses and are actually desirable for some dishes. The frugal practice of using up every scrap of tortilla has its origins in how much work the darn things are to make by hand. Even now, with the store-bought specimens widely available, some of these thrifty dishes taste just as good—and cost almost as little—as they once did.

## Toasting Cumin

T O AVOID OVERBROWNING THE CUMIN (AND DESTROYING THE SOUGHT-AFTER NUTTY TASTE), begin with a generous quantity of seeds— half a cup or so. Place the seeds in a small heavy skillet over low heat and cook, stirring often, until browned and fragrant (some seeds may pop), 7 or 8 minutes. Remove from the skillet immediately and cool. Store the toasted seeds airtight and grind them when needed in an electric spice mill or in a mortar with a pestle.

# Tostaditas

**W**ARM, FRESHLY FRIED TORTILLA CHIPS, ESPECIALLY WHEN PREPARED FROM HOMEMADE TORTILLAS, are so full of toasty corn flavor that they hardly need a dip. You may never again buy a bag of factory-made chips, oversalted and often stale. A dozen 6-inch tortillas will make enough for four to six people.

12 6-inch yellow, blue, or chile-flavored (page 8) corn tortillas

About 4 cups corn or peanut oil, for deep-frying
Salt

Stack the tortillas together 4 at a time and, with a knife, cut them into 6 equal wedges. Spread the tortillas on the work surface for 15 to 20 minutes to dry them slightly.

In an electric deep-fryer or in a medium heavy saucepan fitted with a frying thermometer and set over moderate heat, warm the oil to between 375° and 400°F. (The fryer or pan should be no more than half full.) Working in batches to avoid overcrowding the fryer, cook the tortilla wedges, stirring them once or twice, until they are crisp but not browned, about 1 minute. With a slotted spoon, transfer the tostaditas to paper towels to drain. Sprinkle them lightly with salt to taste. Serve warm.

Note: The tostaditas can be prepared up to 8 hours ahead and stored at room temperature in a closed paper bag. If you want to serve them warm, spread on baking sheets and bake in a preheated 250°F oven until heated through, 5 to 10 minutes.

Baked Tostaditas: Preheat the oven to 350°F. Spread the cut tortillas on an ungreased baking sheet. Spray the tortillas lightly with nonstick vegetable spray. Bake for 6 minutes. Turn the tostaditas, spray again, and continue baking until they are golden and crisp, about 3 minutes.

# Black Bean Nachos with Grilled Shrimp "Salsa"

NACHOS CAN BE FOUND ALL OVER THE COUNTRY (SOMETIMES IN WOEBEGONE VERSIONS that make me wish the recipe had stayed in Texas, where we could protect it from harm), but rarely as upscale as this rendition.

¼ cup fresh lime juice

2 tablespoons olive oil

2 tablespoons tequila

1 ½ teaspoons ground cumin, preferably from toasted seeds (page 13)

1 garlic clove, peeled and crushed

¾ teaspoon salt

1 pound (about 24) large shrimp, shelled and deveined

1 cup wood smoking chips, preferably mesquite, soaked in water for at least 30 minutes

1 medium tomato, cored and diced

2 large fresh jalapeños, stemmed and minced

3 green onions, trimmed and thinly sliced (green tops included)

3 tablespoons minced cilantro

36 Tostaditas (page 15) or packaged unspiced thick corn tortilla chips

¾ cup refried pinto or black beans, homemade (page 55) or canned

2 ½ cups grated medium Cheddar or Monterey Jack cheese, or a combination

In a medium bowl, whisk together 2 tablespoons of the lime juice, the olive oil, tequila, cumin, garlic, and ½ teaspoon of the salt. Add the shrimp and marinate, stirring once or twice, for 1 hour. Drain the shrimp, reserving the marinade, and slide them onto 3 or 4 flat metal skewers.

Prepare a charcoal fire and let it burn down until the coals are evenly white or preheat a gas grill (medium-high). Drain the wood chips and scatter them over the hot coals or lava stones. Position the rack about 6 inches above the heat source.

When the wood chips are smoking heavily, lay the skewers on the grill, cover, and cook, basting with the reserved marinade and turning the skewers once, until the shrimp are pink, curled, and just cooked through, about 4 minutes total. Remove the shrimp from the grill, cool slightly, and slide them off the skewers.

Coarsely chop the shrimp. In a medium bowl, combine the shrimp, tomato, jalapeños, green onions, cilantro, remaining 2 tablespoons lime juice, and remaining ¼ teaspoon salt. Let stand at room temperature for 30 minutes.    (continued)

Meanwhile, position racks in the upper and lower thirds of the oven and preheat to 450°F. Spread each tostadita with about 1 teaspoon of refried beans and arrange the tostaditas in a single layer on 1 or 2 heatproof serving platters. Sprinkle the cheese evenly over the tostaditas.

Bake, exchanging the positions of the plates on the racks if necessary, until the cheese is melted and the nachos are sizzling, about 5 minutes.

Working quickly, spoon about 1 tablespoon of the shrimp salsa, including juices, onto each nacho. Serve immediately.

## Two-Cheese Quesadillas with Hot Cherry Pepper

MAKES 4 TO 6 APPETIZER SERVINGS

**H**OT CHERRY PEPPERS (FOUND IN THE PICKLE SECTION OF THE MARKET) are often overlooked in favor of other peppers like jalapeños. They add their own brand of sweet zing to this quesadilla. A quesadilla makes a great lunch, but here it is cut into wedges to become a surefire appetizer.

4 8-inch flour tortillas
1/2 pound goat cheese, softened
1 cup cooked and drained black beans
4 large jarred hot cherry peppers, stemmed and thinly sliced

2 green onions, trimmed and thinly sliced
1/4 pound Monterey Jack cheese, grated
Nonstick spray
Sour cream, Guacamole (page 40), and salsa (optional)

Lay a tortilla on a flat cookie sheet. Spread it evenly with half the goat cheese. Scatter half the beans, cherry peppers, green onions, and Monterey Jack over the goat cheese. Top with a second tortilla.

Set a large heavy skillet, preferably nonstick, over medium-low heat. Spray it with nonstick spray. Slide the quesadilla into the skillet, weight it with a small plate, and cook it until the bottom is crisp and lightly browned, about 3 minutes. Spray the top tortilla lightly with nonstick spray. With a wide spatula, turn the quesadilla. Weight it with the plate and cook another 2 to 3 minutes, or until the bottom is crisp and brown and the cheeses are melted. Slide the quesadilla onto a cutting board, cut into 6 wedges and serve immediately, accompanied by sour cream, guacamole, and salsa.

Repeat with the remaining ingredients.

# Migas with Bacon

A RECIPE THAT USES UP EVERY LAST SCRAP OF YESTERDAY'S TORTILLAS, these pumped-up scrambled eggs (called *migas*) will supply enough fuel to keep you going all morning long and probably a good part of the afternoon too.

2 cups corn oil

6 medium corn tortillas cut into random
  1-inch pieces

Salt

12 eggs

3/4 teaspoon *freshly ground black pepper*

2 tablespoons bacon drippings or
  unsalted butter

12 strips *thick-cut bacon fried crisp*

About 1 1/3 cups hot salsa

In a large skillet over medium heat, warm the oil. Working in batches, fry the tortilla pieces until crisp, about 2 minutes. Transfer with a slotted spoon to paper towels and sprinkle lightly with salt. *(The tortilla pieces can be fried up to 1 day ahead. Cool completely, wrap airtight, and store at room temperature.)*

In a large bowl, whisk together the eggs, pepper, and 3/4 teaspoon salt. In a large heavy skillet, preferably nonstick, warm the bacon fat over medium heat. Add the eggs and tortilla pieces and cook, stirring often, until the eggs are done to your liking, about 4 minutes for medium-firm (the tortilla pieces will become soggy).

Divide the eggs among 4 plates. Arrange the bacon strips around the eggs. Top the eggs with salsa and serve immediately.

# My Tortilla Soup

MAKES 6 SERVINGS

**I** DEVISED THIS CHUNKY TOMATO-CHICKEN SOUP, MADE EVEN THICKER WITH TORTILLA STRIPS THAT SOAK UP THE BROTH, to be served as a main course. If you can't find a can of chopped tomatoes with green chiles (Rotel brand is in practically every southwestern supermarket, but it's not so easy to find elsewhere), use ¾ cup chopped canned tomatoes mixed with 2 tablespoons canned chopped mild green chiles.

About 4 cups corn or peanut oil

9 6-inch yellow, blue, or chile-flavored (page 8) corn tortillas, cut into strips

2 tablespoons olive oil

1 3¼-pound chicken, cut into serving pieces, with giblets (but not the liver)

3 cups chopped yellow onions

3 medium carrots, peeled and chopped

8 garlic cloves, peeled and chopped

¾ teaspoon dried oregano, crumbled

¾ teaspoon dried marjoram, crumbled

2 bay leaves

4 cups lightly salted chicken broth

4 cups water

1 10-ounce can chopped tomatoes with green chiles

3 chipotles en adobo, with clinging sauce, minced

2 cups cooked and drained chickpeas

1 ⅓ cups frozen green peas, thawed and drained

Salt

2 cups coarsely chopped fresh spinach leaves

In an electric deep-fryer or in a medium heavy saucepan fitted with a frying thermometer and set over moderate heat, warm the corn oil to between 375° and 400°F. (The fryer or pan should be no more than half full.) Working in batches to avoid overcrowding the fryer, cook the tortilla strips, stirring them once or twice, until they are crisp but not browned, about 1 minute. With a slotted spoon, transfer the strips to paper towels to drain. *(The tortilla strips can be fried up to 1 day ahead; cool completely, then wrap airtight and store at room temperature.)*

In a heavy 5-quart soup pot over medium heat, warm the olive oil. Pat the chicken pieces dry. Working in batches, cook the chicken pieces and giblets, turning them occasionally, until lightly browned, about 10 minutes. Transfer to a plate. Add the onions, carrots, garlic, oregano, marjoram, and bay leaves to the pan and cook, covered, stirring occasionally and scraping the bottom of the pan, for 10 minutes.

Return the chicken pieces to the pan. Add the broth, water, tomatoes, and chipotles and bring to a simmer. Cook, partially covered, for 20 minutes. Remove the white meat pieces and reserve. Cook another 5 to 10 minutes. Remove the dark meat pieces. When the chicken is cool enough to handle, remove and discard the skin; remove the meat from the bones and shred it slightly. Return the chicken to the pot. *(The soup can be prepared to this point 2 days in advance. Cool completely and refrigerate.)*

Set the soup over medium heat. Add the chickpeas and green peas and bring to a simmer. Cook 5 minutes, stirring often. Remove from the heat and add salt to taste. Stir in the spinach. Ladle the soup into bowls. Top each bowl with tortilla strips, dividing them evenly and using them all. Serve immediately.

# Willy's Tortilla Club Sandwich

MAKES 2 SERVINGS

**I**RUSTLED THIS RECIPE FROM WILLY'S, A SELF-STYLED "SLEAZY" CANTINA IN SANTA FE. You may never want a club sandwich on boring old toast again, but if you really miss the frilly toothpicks, go ahead and stick them in this twist on the quesadilla theme.

*Nonstick spray*
*3 8-inch flour tortillas*
*About 3 tablespoons mayonnaise*
*¼ pound thinly sliced roast turkey*

*½ cup grated jalapeño Jack cheese*
*3 thin slices ripe tomato*
*4 crisp strips bacon*

Preheat the oven to 400°F. Spray a baking sheet lightly with nonstick spray. Lay a tortilla on the baking sheet. Spread the tortilla evenly with 1 tablespoon of the mayonnaise. Arrange the turkey over the mayonnaise. Sprinkle half the grated cheese over the turkey. Spread another tortilla with 1 tablespoon mayonnaise and invert it over the grated cheese. Spread the upper side of the second tortilla with the remaining mayonnaise. Lay the tomato slices over the mayonnaise; arrange the bacon strips over the tomatoes. Sprinkle the remaining cheese evenly over all. Lay the remaining tortilla atop this stack and cover with foil. Weight the sandwich with a pot lid or an oven-proof plate or dish.

Bake until the cheese has melted and the remaining ingredients are heated through, about 15 minutes. Transfer to a cutting board and cut into 4 wedges. Transfer 2 wedges to each of 2 plates and serve immediately.

# Roast Chicken with Fruited Corn Tortilla Stuffing

MAKES 4 TO 6 SERVINGS

**D**AY-OLD, SLIGHTLY DRY TORTILLAS NEVER GO TO WASTE IN THE TEX-MEX KITCHEN. Here they are added to a luscious apricot, chorizo, and green chile bread stuffing.

¾ pound Mexican-style (spicy, unsmoked) chorizo sausage

4 tablespoons olive oil

1 cup chopped yellow onions

3 cups day-old (but not dry) corn tortillas torn into small pieces (about 8 medium tortillas)

3 cups day-old (but not dry) firm white peasant-style sourdough bread cut in ½-inch cubes

1 cup (about 4 ounces) coarsely chopped dried apricots

6 long green chiles, roasted, peeled, and chopped (page 31), or 1 cup frozen chopped roasted green chiles, thawed and drained

1 ¼ cups lightly salted chicken broth

1 egg, well beaten

Freshly ground black pepper

1 4- to 4 ½-pound roasting chicken

Salt

Crumble the chorizo into a cold skillet, set it over medium heat, and cook, stirring, until lightly browned, about 10 minutes. With a slotted spoon, transfer the sausage to paper towels to drain. Discard the drippings and wipe the skillet.

Set the skillet over medium heat. Add 3 tablespoons of the oil and the onions and cook, uncovered, stirring occasionally, until lightly browned, about 7 minutes. Cool.

Position a rack in the middle of the oven and preheat to 400°F. In a medium bowl, combine the tortillas, bread cubes, apricots, green chiles, chorizo, and the onions with their oil. Add the broth and egg and stir. Season generously with fresh pepper and stir again.

Spoon the stuffing into the cavity of the chicken, packing it lightly. Pat the chicken dry and set it on a rack in a shallow roasting pan. Rub the skin with the remaining 1 tablespoon olive oil and sprinkle lightly with salt and pepper.

Roast the chicken until it is crisp and brown and the juices from a thigh, when pricked at its thickest, run pinkish yellow, 1 hour 10 minutes to 1 hour 20 minutes. Let the chicken stand on a rack, tented with foil, for 20 minutes.

Spoon the stuffing out of the chicken and out of the bowl into a serving dish. Carve the chicken and serve immediately, accompanied by the stuffing.

# Grilled Tuna Salad Tostadas

**F**ISH TACOS ARE SELLING LIKE HOTCAKES ON THE WEST COAST, SO WHY NOT TUNA TOSTADAS? or swordfish steaks.

1 ½ cups hot green salsa

2 tablespoons tequila

2 thick (1 ½-inch) skinless tuna steaks (about 1 ¼ pounds total)

1 cup wood smoking chips, preferably mesquite, soaked in water for at least 30 minutes

About 1 cup corn oil

4 6-inch yellow or blue corn tortillas

Salt

1 buttery-ripe California avocado, pitted, peeled, and cut into ½-inch cubes

⅓ cup diced red onions

2 pickled jalapeños, stemmed and minced

3 tablespoons minced cilantro

1 ½ tablespoons fresh lime juice

1 ⅓ cups refried black or pinto beans, homemade (page 55) or canned, heated

1 ⅓ cups grated Monterey Jack cheese

2 cups finely shredded romaine lettuce

1 medium red-ripe tomato (about 6 ounces), cored and diced

In a shallow nonreactive dish, stir together ¾ cup of the salsa and the tequila. Add the tuna steaks, cover, and marinate, turning once or twice, for 1 hour.

Light a charcoal fire and let it burn down until the coals are evenly white or preheat a gas grill (medium). Drain the wood chips and scatter them over the hot coals or lava stones. Position the grill rack about 6 inches above the heat source. When the chips are smoking heavily, place the tuna steaks on the grill (reserving the marinade). Cover and grill, turning once or twice and basting with the marinade, until almost cooked but still pink at the center, about 10 minutes. Remove from the grill.

In a large skillet over medium heat, warm the corn oil. When it is hot, add the tortillas, working in batches, and cook them, turning once or twice, until they are crisp, about 1 minute. Transfer to paper towels to drain. Season lightly with salt.

Cut the tuna into ½-inch cubes. In a medium bowl, combine the tuna, the remaining ¾ cup salsa, and the avocado, onions, jalapeños, cilantro, lime juice, and ½ teaspoon salt. Toss gently.

Spread the beans evenly over the fried tortillas. Sprinkle the cheese evenly over the beans. Mound the lettuce on top of the cheese and spoon the tuna salad evenly over the lettuce. Drizzle any juices from the bowl over the salad. Garnish with tomato.

# Burritos Desayunos

**W**HAT DO YOU MEAN YOU'VE NEVER HAD A BURRITO FOR BREAKFAST? My recipe is just a blueprint for your own creativity, the only constants being eggs and flour tortillas. Stuff yours with cooked bacon, ham, or chorizo and, if you have a hankering, home-fried potatoes too.

10 eggs
1/2 teaspoon salt
1/2 teaspoon freshly ground black pepper
1 cup refried black or pinto beans, home-made (page 55) or canned
4 10-inch flour tortillas

2 tablespoons unsalted butter
1/3 cup sliced green onions
1/2 pound grated Monterey Jack cheese
1 1/2 cups Green Chile Sauce (page 56) or Red Chile Pod Sauce (page 58), heated to simmering

Position racks in the upper and lower thirds of the oven and preheat to 350°F.

In a large bowl, whisk together the eggs, salt, and pepper. Spread 1/4 cup of the refried beans in a 5-inch round in the middle of each tortilla. Lay the tortillas on 2 baking sheets and warm them in the oven.

Meanwhile, in a large heavy skillet, preferably nonstick, melt the butter over medium heat. Add the green onions and cook 1 minute. Add the eggs and cook, stirring often, until done to your liking, about 4 minutes for medium-firm. Remove the skillet from the heat and stir the cheese into the eggs.

Spoon one-quarter of the egg mixture onto the round of beans on each tortilla. Fold over the edges of each tortilla, then roll up from the bottom to enclose the filling. Transfer each burrito to a plate. Spoon the chile sauce over the tortillas, dividing it evenly and using it all. Serve immediately.

# Chicken Mole Sopa Seca

MAKES 6 TO 8 SERVINGS

**M**EXICAN SOPAS SECAS (LITERALLY "DRY SOUPS") ARE NOT SOUPS AT ALL BUT SPOONABLE CASSEROLES. Here's one of my favorites, made with store-bought mole sauce (see Mail-Order Sources, page 61), shredded chicken, beans, and a good heaping of sour cream.

1 ½ cups corn oil

17 6-inch flour tortillas

1 8 ¼ -ounces jar prepared mole poblano paste

2 ¼ cups lightly salted chicken broth

4 ½ cups cooked and drained black beans

12 ounces Monterey Jack cheese, grated

4 cups Chicken Deshebrada (page 60)

1 cup finely chopped yellow onions

2 cups sour cream

In a large skillet over medium heat, warm the corn oil. Using tongs, dip the tortillas, one at a time, into the oil. Immerse them for about 1 minute; the tortillas should become tender and limp, but not brown or crisp. Drain on paper towels.

Position a rack in the middle of the oven and preheat to 375°F.

In a small saucepan, set the mole paste over low heat. Gradually whisk 2 cups of the chicken broth into the paste; the mixture should be smooth. Remove from the heat and keep warm.

In a bowl, roughly mash the beans with a fork. Stir in the remaining ¼ cup chicken broth.

Arrange 5 tortillas, overlapping them slightly, over the bottom and partway up the sides of a deep 4 ½-quart covered baking dish. Spread half the bean mixture over the tortillas. Sprinkle one-third of the cheese over the beans. Arrange 3 tortillas, overlapping them, on top of the cheese. Sprinkle half the chicken over the tortillas; scatter half the onions over the chicken. Spread half the sour cream over the onions. Spoon half the mole over the sour cream, tilting the casserole to encourage it to run down into the layers.

Arrange 3 tortillas on top of the mole, overlapping them. Repeat the layering procedure. Arrange the last 3 tortillas on top of the mole, overlapping them. Spread the remaining sour cream over the tortillas; sprinkle the remaining cheese on top.

Cover the dish and bake for 40 minutes. Uncover and bake until the top is browned and the sopa is piping hot and bubbling, about 20 minutes. Let rest on a rack for 10 minutes before serving.

# Roasting Chiles

**F**IRE-ROASTING CHILES LOOSENS THEIR TOUGH, RATHER INDI-GESTIBLE PEELS, partially cooks the flesh, and adds a smoky flavor. When roasted directly on the burner grids of a gas range, the chiles will be slightly crunchy. If roasted under the broiler, on a stovetop chile-roasting rack that sits over an electric or gas burner, or on an outdoor grill, the chiles will be softer.

Pierce the chiles near their stems with the tip of a knife. Roast or broil the chiles, turning them two or three times as they blacken, until the peels are lightly but evenly charred (the appearance of white ash is a sign the chiles have been overroasted, leading to some loss of flesh). Steam the chiles in a closed paper bag or in a covered bowl until cool. Rub away the burned peel. Wipe the chiles with paper towels to remove as much of the peel as possible, but avoid rinsing the chiles, which washes away flavor.

Stem and seed the chiles and trim off the inner ribs. Chop or julienne the chiles as needed for the recipe.

Chiles may also be peeled by dipping them briefly into hot (375°F) oil, but this method does not add a smoky flavor. Cover and cook, then peel as directed above.

# Freezing Roasted Chiles

**F**REEZING IS ONE OF THE BEST WAYS TO PRESERVE THE FLEET-ING, SEASONAL PERFECTION OF FIELD-RIPENED FRESH CHILES. After fire-roasting (see above), the chiles are merely cooled, not peeled, and packed, six or so at a time, into plastic freezer bags. Defrost and peel the chiles before using. They will keep for up to one year.

# Chilaquiles

MAKES 8 SERVINGS

CHILAQUILES (WHICH MEANS "BROKEN SOMBRERO," REFERRING TO THE SHAPE OF THE TORTILLA PIECES) is a beloved cheese and tortilla dish. Whether I serve it for brunch (with a big bowl of freshly scrambled eggs) or supper (with a green salad), it is the kind of comfort food that will make a Mexican grownup long for Mamacita's home cooking.

4 cups corn oil

27 5-inch day-old (but not dry) corn tortillas, quartered

Salt

1 recipe Red Chile Pod Sauce (page 58)

3 cups grated medium-sharp Cheddar or Monterey Jack cheese, or a combination of both

1 cup finely chopped yellow onions

2 cups sour cream

In a large skillet over medium heat, warm the oil. Working in batches, add the tortilla quarters to the oil and fry, turning them once or twice, until partially crisp, about 3 minutes; the tortillas should not brown and should remain slightly leathery and flexible. With a slotted spoon, transfer to paper towels to drain. Season lightly with salt. (The tortillas can be fried up to 1 day ahead. Wrap airtight and store at room temperature.)

Position a rack in the middle of the oven and preheat to 375°F. Spread 1 cup of the chile sauce over the bottom of a 9 x 13-inch baking dish. Arrange about one-third of the tortilla pieces over the sauce (try for a single layer, but there will be some overlapping). Drizzle the tortilla pieces with 1/2 cup sauce, then sprinkle them with 1 cup cheese and half the onions. Arrange half the remaining tortilla pieces over the onions. Drizzle with 1/2 cup sauce, then sprinkle them with half the remaining cheese and all the remaining onions. Top the onions with a final layer of tortilla pieces. Pour the remaining chile sauce evenly over the tortilla pieces. Sprinkle the sauce with the remaining cheese. Dollop the sour cream over the cheese and, with the back of a spoon, smooth it into an even layer.

Bake the chilaquiles until the top is lightly browned and the sauce and cheese are bubbling, about 35 minutes. Let stand on a rack for 5 minutes before serving.

# Pork and Green Chile Flautas

MAKES 4 TO 6 SERVINGS

**Y**OU'VE HEARD OF FINGER-LICKIN' GOOD? WELL, DIPPING CRISP PORK AND CHILE FLAUTAS INTO CREMA OR GUACAMOLE is more like finger-lickin' *incredible!* Of course, you can use Chicken Deshebrada (page 60) for the filling if you wish.

12 6-inch corn tortillas
4 cups Pork Deshebrada (page 59)
6 long green chiles, roasted, peeled
  (page 31), and cut into julienne strips
Salt

About 2 cups corn oil
4 cups finely shredded romaine lettuce
Crema (page 50) or Guacamole (page 40)
Hot green or red salsa

Lay a corn tortilla on the work surface. Arrange about ⅓ cup of the shredded pork and about one-twelfth of the julienned chiles across the lower third of the tortilla. Season with a pinch of salt and roll the tortilla into a tube about 1 inch in diameter. Secure with a toothpick. Repeat with the remaining ingredients, producing 12 flautas.

In a large deep skillet, warm about ½ inch of corn oil over medium heat. Add the flautas, working in batches if necessary, and fry them, turning once, until they are almost (but not quite) crisp, about 2 minutes per side. With tongs, transfer the flautas to paper towels, propping them against something (an inverted cake tin is ideal) to drain them thoroughly.

Layer the shredded romaine on 4 to 6 plates. Arrange 2 or 3 flautas on top of the romaine. Serve immediately, accompanied by crema or guacamole and salsa for dipping.

# Chili con Carne Tostada Compuestas

**O**NCE YOU'VE PREPARED CRUNCHY TORTILLA CUPS (SEE THE MAIL-ORDER SOURCES, PAGE 61, to purchase the specially designed double baskets to form the cups), you can fill them with whatever tickles your fancy. Here good old chili con carne is turned into a dish fit for a fiesta.

8 Corn Tortilla Cups (recipe follows)

4 cups chili con carne, heated to simmering

3 cups grated medium-sharp Cheddar cheese (about ¾ pound)

3 cups shredded romaine lettuce

2 medium tomatoes (about 1 pound total), cored, seeded, and diced

1 ½ cups sour cream

1 cup chopped yellow onions

Position a rack in the middle of the oven and preheat to 300°F.

Arrange the tortilla cups on a baking sheet and set them in the oven until heated through, about 5 minutes. Set 2 tortilla cups on each of 4 plates. Divide the chili among the cups. Top the chili with the cheese, lettuce, and tomatoes. Dollop the sour cream on top of the tomatoes. Sprinkle the onions over all and serve immediately.

## Corn Tortilla Cups
(MAKES 8)

About 4 cups corn oil          8 thin 6-inch corn tortillas          Salt

In a deep-fryer or in a deep heavy pan fitted with a frying thermometer, warm the corn oil. At about 200°F, dip each tortilla briefly into the oil; the oil should not bubble and the tortilla should become tender and flexible but should not begin to crisp. Drain on paper towels.

When the oil reaches 375°F, dip both halves of a corn tortilla frying basket into the oil. Place a tortilla between the halves, fit them together, lower the tortilla basket into the hot oil, and fry about 1 minute, or until crisp. Carefully remove the tortilla cup from the basket and transfer it to absorbent paper. Season it lightly with salt. Repeat with the remaining tortillas. *(The tortilla cups can be prepared several days ahead. Store airtight at room temperature for up to a week.)*

# Turkey Picadillo Chimichangas

MAKES 8 SERVINGS

**P**ICADILLO, A SPICY MIXTURE OF GROUND MEAT, ALMONDS, AND OLIVES, IS ONE OF THOSE ALL-PURPOSE FILLINGS that the Mexican cook needs to master in order to whip up family meals in a hurry. It is often made with pork or beef, but I like the versatile, mild taste of ground turkey. Buy the thinnest, largest (at least 10 inches in diameter) flour tortillas you can find for the best chimichangas.

2 tablespoons olive oil

1 cup chopped yellow onions

4 garlic cloves, peeled and minced

2 teaspoons dried oregano, crumbled

1 teaspoon ground cumin, preferably from toasted seeds (page 13)

1/2 teaspoon ground cinnamon

2 pounds ground turkey

1 teaspoon salt

2 cups Green Chile Sauce (page 56), Red Chile Pod Sauce (page 58), or canned green or red enchilada sauce

1/2 cup lightly salted chicken broth

1 medium tomato, cored and chopped

1/3 cup dark raisins

1/4 cup sliced pimiento-stuffed small green olives

1 teaspoon freshly ground black pepper

8 10-inch thin flour tortillas

About 4 cups corn oil

8 cups shredded romaine lettuce

Hot salsa and sour cream, as accompaniments

In a large skillet over medium heat, warm the olive oil. Add the onions, garlic, oregano, cumin, and cinnamon and cook, covered, stirring once or twice, for 10 minutes. Add the turkey and salt and cook, uncovered, breaking up the meat, until it loses its pink color, about 10 minutes. Add the green chile sauce, chicken broth, tomato, raisins, olives, and pepper and bring to a simmer. Cook, uncovered, stirring occasionally, until thick, about 25 minutes. Remove from the heat and cool to room temperature. *(The turkey mixture can be prepared up to 2 days ahead. Cover and refrigerate, returning it to room temperature before proceeding.)*

Lay a tortilla on the work surface. Spoon 1 cup of the turkey mixture across the middle two-thirds of the tortilla. Fold in the sides, then roll up the tortilla, tightly enclosing the filling; secure with 3 long toothpicks. Repeat with the remaining tortillas and filling. *(The chimichangas can be prepared to this point up to 1 hour before cooking. Cover loosely and hold at room temperature.)*   (continued)

Position a rack in the middle of the oven and preheat to 300°F. In a large deep skillet over medium-high heat, warm the corn oil. Working in batches, fry the chimichangas in the oil, turning them once or twice, until crisp and brown on all sides, about 10 minutes. Transfer the chimichangas to a baking pan lined with paper towels and keep warm in the oven until all are fried.

Divide the lettuce among 8 plates. Place a chimichanga on top of the lettuce on each plate and serve immediately, accompanied by salsa and sour cream.

# Guacamole

MAKES ABOUT 2 CUPS

¾ cup chopped cilantro
1 ½ fresh jalapeños, stemmed and
   chopped
¾ teaspoon salt

3 large ripe California avocados,
   pitted and peeled
¾ pound (3 or 4) ripe Italian-style
   plum tomatoes, diced
⅓ cup diced yellow or red onions

In a mini food processor, purée together the cilantro, jalapeños, and salt. In a medium bowl, roughly mash the avocados. Stir in the cilantro purée, tomatoes, and onions. Adjust the seasonings. (*The guacamole can be prepared up to 3 hours ahead. Cover it with plastic wrap, pressing the film onto the surface of the guacamole, and refrigerate.*)

# Blue Corn~Black Bean Enchiladas con Huevos

MAKES 4 SERVINGS

**V**EGETARIAN OR NOT, YOUR GUESTS WILL LOVE THESE MEAT-LESS ENCHILADAS, which are layered into individual portions, rather than rolled up.

*About 1 cup corn oil*

*12 6-inch blue corn tortillas*

*4 cups (1 recipe) Red Chile Pod Sauce (page 58)*

*1 1/2 cups cooked and drained black beans*

*3 cups grated Monterey Jack cheese (about 3/4 pound)*

*1/2 cup minced yellow onions*

*3 tablespoons unsalted butter*

*4 eggs*

*Salt*

*Freshly ground black pepper*

*2 cups shredded romaine lettuce*

Position a rack in the middle of the oven and preheat to 375°F.

In a medium skillet, warm 1/2 inch of corn oil over moderate heat. Using tongs, dip the tortillas, one at a time, into the oil, turn them, and then transfer to paper towels to drain. The tortillas should be in the oil no more than 30 seconds or so, and the oil should be hot enough to soften them but not so hot that their edges begin to crisp.

Spread about 1/2 cup of the chile sauce in the bottom of a shallow baking dish just large enough to hold 4 tortillas in a single layer without overlapping. (Or use 4 individual round gratin dishes.)

One at a time, dip the tortillas into the chile sauce. Transfer the dipped tortillas to the baking dish, arranging them in a single layer. Spoon about 3 tablespoons of the beans over each tortilla. Sprinkle about 1/4 cup of the cheese over the beans. Sprinkle about 1 tablespoon of the onions over the cheese. Repeat dipping and layering the tortillas, topping each layer with beans, cheese, and onions. Pour any remaining sauce over the enchiladas. Sprinkle any remaining cheese and onions over the sauce. Bake the enchiladas for 8 to 10 minutes, or until the cheese is melted and the sauce is heated through and bubbling.

In a large skillet melt the butter. Break the eggs into the butter, cover the skillet, and cook until the eggs are set but not hard, about 4 minutes. Season the eggs with salt and pepper to taste.

With a wide spatula, transfer each enchilada stack to a heated plate. Top each stack with a fried egg. Garnish each plate with a mound of romaine and serve immediately.

# Soft Corn Tacos with Potatoes and Mushrooms

MAKES 8 TACOS

**I**FEEL SORRY FOR THOSE PEOPLE OUT THERE WHO THINK THAT A TACO is a hard, curved yellow Frisbee filled with some brown meat. Soft tacos are a treat, and this imaginative filling is miles away from what you'll find in a fast food restaurant.

1 ½ pounds (about 3 medium) red-skinned
   potatoes
4 tablespoons olive oil
3 long green chiles, roasted, peeled
   (page 31), and cut into julienne strips
1 large sweet red pepper, roasted, peeled
   (page 31), and cut into julienne strips
4 garlic cloves, peeled and chopped
1 pound fresh shiitake mushrooms,
   stemmed and cut into ¼-inch slices

1 ½ teaspoons salt
½ cup Crema (page 50), crème
   fraîche, or sour cream
¼ cup minced cilantro
1 medium yellow onion, peeled and sliced
¾ teaspoon toasted cumin seeds (page 13)
½ teaspoon freshly ground black pepper
8 6-inch corn tortillas

In a medium pan, cover the potatoes with cold water. Set over medium heat and bring to a boil. Cook, partially covered, until the potatoes are tender, about 35 minutes. Drain and cool. Peel the potatoes and cut into ½-inch cubes.

In a large skillet over medium heat, warm 2 tablespoons of the olive oil. Add the green chiles, red pepper, and garlic and cook, covered, stirring once or twice, for 5 minutes. Add the shiitakes and 1 teaspoon of the salt, cover, and cook, stirring once or twice, for 7 minutes; the mushrooms will give up their juices and soften. Stir in the crema and the cilantro and simmer until heated through, about 2 minutes (if using sour cream, do not simmer).

Meanwhile, in a large skillet over medium heat, warm the remaining 2 tablespoons oil. Add the onion and cumin seeds and cook, covered, stirring once or twice, for 5 minutes. Add the cubed potatoes and season with the remaining ½ teaspoon salt and the pepper. Raise the heat slightly and cook, stirring often, until the potatoes and onions are lightly browned, 5 to 7 minutes.

Working in batches, on a heated dry griddle (or heavy skillet), warm the tortillas, turning them once or twice, until they are fragrant and flexible, about 20 seconds. Put 2 tortillas on each of 4 plates. Divide the potato mixture evenly among the tortillas; divide the mushroom mixture evenly over the potatoes. Serve immediately.

# Oven-Barbecued Brisket Tacos

WHEN IS A STUFFED FLOUR TORTILLA NOT A BURRITO? BURRITOS NORMALLY HAVE A REFRIED BEAN BASE with meat and other goodies added, whereas tacos (hard or soft) have fewer ingredients. And when the filling is this tangy, meltingly tender barbecued brisket, your mouth wouldn't want any other distractions like beans anyway. If possible, have the butcher give you the thicker "second cut" of brisket rather than the leaner "first cut," as the extra fat will give you a more tender brisket.

2 cups hot and smoky tomato-based
   barbecue sauce
1 cup dark beer
1 cup lightly salted beef broth
2 tablespoons unblended medium-hot
   powdered red chiles, preferably from
   Chimayo or Dixon, New Mexico

1 tablespoon hot pepper sauce
1 tablespoon Worcestershire sauce
1 5-pound beef brisket
1 large onion, peeled and sliced
16 soft 6-inch flour tortillas

Position a rack in the middle of the oven and preheat to 325°F.

In a medium bowl, whisk together the barbecue sauce, beer, broth, powdered chiles, pepper sauce, and Worcestershire sauce.

Pierce and flour a large (holding up to 12 pounds) brown-in bag according to the manufacturer's directions. Lay the brisket, fat side up, in the bag and put the bag in a shallow baking dish just large enough to hold it. Scatter the onion over the brisket and pour the barbecue mixture on top. Seal the bag.

Bake the brisket for about 4 1/2 hours, or until it is tender and the sauce has thickened. Let the brisket rest in the bag in the pan on a rack for 10 minutes. Increase the oven temperature to 400°F.

Transfer the brisket to a cutting board. Scrape any barbecue sauce from the bag over the meat. Cut the meat across the grain and at a slight angle into thin slices. Transfer the sliced brisket to a heated platter.

Meanwhile, working in batches, lay the flour tortillas directly on the oven rack for 10 to 20 seconds, or until they are heated through and lightly marked but still flexible. Transfer the tortillas to a napkin-lined basket. Serve the brisket and tortillas immediately.

# West Texas Beef Fajitas

MAKES 6 SERVINGS

**Y**EOW, THIS IS SOME MARINADE! BEER, TEQUILA, SALSA—IF YOU DON'T FEEL LIKE MAKING THE FAJITAS, just add some tortilla chips and maracas and have a party! This is a schizophrenic, indoor-outdoor recipe: the meat is grilled over mesquite, but the all-important onion-pepper mixture is sizzled indoors in a skillet. The vegetables can be made ahead, wrapped in a foil packet, and reheated over the coals if you want to assemble the meal outdoors.

1 cup tomato-based pico de gallo (refrigerated fresh salsa) or bottled hot salsa,
  plus additional to accompany the fajitas
1/2 cup chopped red onions
1/2 cup packed fresh cilantro
  (stems can be included)
4 tablespoons olive oil
3 chipotles en adobo, with clinging sauce
2 tablespoons tequila
2 tablespoons fresh lime juice
1/2 cup dark beer
2 1/2 pounds (2 or 3 pieces) skirt steak

2 medium yellow onions, peeled, halved,
  and thinly sliced
3 large sweet peppers, ideally 1 each
  of red, yellow, and orange
2 teaspoons Worcestershire sauce
1 teaspoon soy sauce
2 cups wood smoking chips, preferably
  mesquite, soaked in water for at least
  30 minutes
18 6-inch flour tortillas
Guacamole (page 40) or sour cream,
  for garnish

In a food processor, purée 1 cup of the pico de gallo with the red onions, cilantro, 2 tablespoons of the olive oil, the chipotles, tequila, and lime juice. Stir in the beer. In a shallow nonreactive dish, pour the marinade over the skirt steak and let it stand at room temperature, covered, turning it once or twice, for 2 hours.

In a large heavy skillet over medium heat, warm the remaining 2 tablespoons of olive oil. Stir in the onions and peppers, season with Worcestershire and soy sauce, and cook, covered, stirring once or twice, for 8 minutes. Uncover, raise the heat to medium-high, and cook, tossing and stirring often, until the vegetables are lightly browned and almost tender, about 5 minutes. Remove from the heat.

Meanwhile, light a charcoal fire and let it burn down until the coals are evenly white or preheat a gas grill (medium). Drain the wood chips and scatter them over the hot coals or lava stones. Position the grill rack about 6 inches above the heat source. Remove the pieces of skirt steak from the marinade (reserving it) and lay them on the grill rack. Cover and cook, basting often with the reserved marinade, for 7 minutes. Turn the steak and continue to cook, basting with the remaining marinade, for another 7 minutes (for medium-rare), or until done to your liking. Transfer the steak to a cutting board and tent with foil. Let rest for 10 minutes.

Meanwhile, reheat the onion-pepper mixture if necessary. Cut the steak across the grain and at a slight angle into thin slices. Transfer to a heated platter and top with the vegetables. Warm the tortillas by turning them briefly on the grill, just until they are lightly marked and flexible but not dry, about 20 seconds. Transfer the tortillas to a napkin-lined basket and serve the fajitas immediately, accompanied by salsa and guacamole or sour cream.

# Crema

MAKES ABOUT 2 CUPS

Tangy crema, or cultured heavy cream, is the Mexican equivalent of French crème fraîche, which can be substituted (look for it in a good cheese shop).

2 cups heavy cream, preferably not
    ultra-pasteurized

3 tablespoons cultured buttermilk
    or plain yogurt

In a bowl, whisk together the heavy cream and buttermilk. Loosely cover and let stand at room temperature for 12 hours; the mixture will thicken and become acidic. Cover and refrigerate until using; the cream will thicken further and become more tart. It will keep for up to 10 days.

# Peach and Pecan Chimichangas with Raspberry Sauce

**T**HESE ARE NOT AS WACKY AS THEY SOUND, BEING KISSING COUSIN TO A FRIED FRUIT PIE (which is more Pennsylvania Dutch than Navajo, but let's not split hairs when something is this delicious). Serving the "chimis" with raspberry sauce and sour cream gives them a professional flourish, but they can be sprinkled with powdered sugar for a more down-home approach.

3 pounds (about 6 medium) just-ripe
  peaches
¹/₂ cup sugar
2 tablespoons fresh lemon juice
1 tablespoon minced lemon zest
  (colored peel)
¹/₂ teaspoon vanilla extract

1 cup pecans
4 10-inch thin flour tortillas
About 4 cups corn oil
Raspberry Sauce (recipe follows)
¹/₄ cup sour cream
Confectioners' sugar

Bring a medium saucepan of water to a boil. Working in batches, lower the peaches into the water, wait 30 seconds, then lift them out with a slotted spoon and transfer them to a bowl of cold water. Drain the peaches. Peel and pit them and coarsely chop the flesh.

In a medium nonreactive saucepan over moderate heat, combine the chopped peaches, sugar, lemon juice, and zest. Cover and bring to a brisk simmer, then uncover and cook, stirring occasionally, until very thick, about 1 hour. Stir in the vanilla and remove from the heat. Cool to room temperature, then refrigerate until very cold, at least 5 hours. *(The peach mixture can be prepared up to 2 days ahead.)*

Position a rack in the middle of the oven and preheat to 375°F. Spread the pecans in a single layer in a metal pan (like a cake tin) and bake, stirring once or twice, until browned and fragrant, 8 to 10 minutes. Remove from the oven, cool, and coarsely chop.

Just before assembling the chimichangas, stir the pecans into the peach mixture. Lay a tortilla on the work surface. Spoon 1 cup of the peach-pecan mixture across the middle two-thirds of the tortilla. Fold in the sides, then roll up the tortilla, tightly enclosing the filling; secure with 3 long toothpicks. Repeat with the remaining tortillas and filling. *(The chimichangas can be prepared to this point up to ¹/₂ hour before cooking. Cover loosely and refrigerate.)* (continued)

In a large deep skillet over medium-high heat, warm the corn oil. Fry the chimi-changas in the oil, turning them once or twice, until crisp and brown on all sides, about 10 minutes. With tongs, transfer to paper towels to drain briefly.

Spoon a generous pool of raspberry sauce onto each of 4 plates. Put 2 dollops of sour cream on the edges of each pool of sauce. Draw the tip of a knife through the sour cream to create a decorative effect. Set the chimichangas on the sauce, dust powdered sugar evenly over the chimichangas and serve immediately.

### Raspberry Sauce
(MAKES ABOUT 1 ¾ CUPS)

3 ½-pint baskets fresh raspberries     2 tablespoons fresh lime juice     About ⅔ cup sugar

In a food processor, combine the raspberries, lime juice, and ½ cup of the sugar. Process until smooth. Force the sauce through a sieve or through the medium blade of a food mill. Cover the sauce and refrigerate until cold. If desired, add additional sugar to taste just before serving.

# Chocolate-Kahlúa Sundaes in Corn Tortilla Cups

MAKES 8 SERVINGS

**I**N TANDEM WITH OTHER MEXICAN FLAVORS LIKE CHOCOLATE, CINNAMON, AND KAHLÚA, the slightly sweet taste of corn is really a nice, compatible surprise in this dessert. Other fillings for the cups work well too—try vanilla ice cream, fresh sliced strawberries, and warm butterscotch topping some other time.

⅓ cup packed light brown sugar
2 tablespoons unsweetened cocoa powder
⅛ teaspoon ground cinnamon
⅛ teaspoon freshly grated nutmeg
8 Corn Tortilla Cups (page 36),
  sprinkled with sugar instead of salt

About 2 pints premium dark chocolate
  ice cream, softened
½ cup Kahlúa (Mexican coffee liqueur)
1 cup heavy cream, whipped to soft peaks

In a small bowl, using your fingertips, work together the brown sugar, cocoa powder, cinnamon, and nutmeg until evenly light and granular.

Set 1 tortilla cup on each of 8 dessert plates. Place 1 generous scoop of ice cream into each tortilla cup. Drizzle 1 tablespoon Kahlúa over each scoop of ice cream. Sprinkle the cocoa mixture evenly over the ice cream, using it all. Top each scoop of ice cream with a dollop of whipped cream and serve immediately.

# "Pot" Beans and Then Refried Beans

✻

MAKES ABOUT 6 SERVINGS OF POT BEANS,
PLUS 6 SERVINGS OF REFRIED BEANS FROM THE LEFTOVERS

WHENEVER I SMELL THE AROMA OF SIMMERING BEANS IN A SOUTHWESTERN KITCHEN, I know some good food isn't far behind. They can be served as a soupy side dish, then mashed and refried the next day as a starchier accompaniment, somewhat like Mexican mashed potatoes.

## Pot Beans

2 pounds dried pinto beans, picked over

3 quarts water

1 ½ cups chopped yellow onions

¼ pound (4 or 5 strips) thick-sliced
   smoky bacon, chopped

1 tablespoon unblended medium-hot
   powdered red chiles preferably from
   Chimayo or Dixon, New Mexico

3 garlic cloves, peeled and chopped

Salt

In a large bowl, soak the beans in cold water for 15 minutes, changing the water 3 times.

In a large pot (tall rather than wide), combine the rinsed beans, 3 quarts of water, the onions, bacon, powdered chiles, and garlic. Bring to a simmer, then partially cover and cook, stirring occasionally, for 2 hours. Stir in 4 teaspoons salt and cook until the beans are very tender and their broth is very thick, another hour or more. Adjust the seasoning and serve immediately. *(The beans can be prepared several days in advance and will improve upon resting. Cool completely, cover, and refrigerate. Rewarm the beans over low heat, stirring often, until simmering.)*

## Refried Beans

2 tablespoons olive oil

6 cups leftover pot beans, with their liquid

Warm the oil in a large nonstick skillet over low heat. Add 1 cup of the beans with liquid and cook, mashing them roughly and stirring often, until thick, about 5 minutes. Repeat, adding beans and liquid 1 cup at a time. The beans are done when they are thick and creamy but not dry. Serve immediately. *(The beans can be refried a few hours in advance. Add the last cup of beans with liquid and immediately remove the skillet from the heat. Partially cover and hold at room temperature. Rewarm over low heat, mashing and stirring until thick and creamy.)*

# Green Chile Sauce

**T**HIS SIMPLE BUT FUNDAMENTAL SAUCE IS THE VERY ESSENCE OF GREEN CHILES, and it's every bit as important to southwestern cooking as, say, basic tomato sauce is to Italian cuisine.

2 tablespoons olive oil

½ cup finely chopped yellow onions

2 garlic cloves, peeled and minced

½ teaspoon dried oregano, crumbled

¼ teaspoon ground cumin, preferably
   from toasted seeds (page 13)

3 tablespoons unbleached all-purpose flour

1 cup lightly salted chicken broth

1 cup water

12 long green chiles (New Mexican or
   Anaheim), roasted, peeled, and chopped
   (page 31) or 2 cups frozen chopped
   green chiles, thawed and drained

¾ teaspoon salt

In a medium heavy saucepan over low heat, warm the olive oil. Add the onions, garlic, oregano, and cumin; cover and cook, stirring once or twice, for 8 minutes. Uncover, stir in the flour, and cook, stirring often, for 2 minutes. Stir in the chicken broth, water, green chiles, and salt and bring to a simmer. Cook, uncovered, stirring occasionally, until thick, about 15 minutes. *(The sauce can be prepared ahead. Cool completely, cover, and refrigerate for up to 3 days or freeze for up to 1 month.)*

# Red Chile Purée

**D**RIED RED CHILES NEED TO BE SOAKED TO RECONSTITUTE THEIR FLESH, then puréed and sieved to remove their tough skins. The resulting crimson paste (which can be refrigerated or frozen) contains the very essence of the chiles, and while not used as is, it is the foundation of many chile-flavored dishes. Here is the method.

6 cups boiling water

¼ pound (about 12 large) mild New Mexico red chile pods, stemmed, seeded, and torn into small pieces

2 chiles de árbol, stemmed and torn into small pieces

1 cup hot tap water

In a medium heat-proof bowl, combine the boiling water with the pieces of chile. Cover and let stand, stirring occasionally, until cool.

Drain, discarding the soaking water. In a food processor, combine the soaked chile pieces with the hot tap water and process, stopping to scrape down the sides of the work bowl once or twice, until smooth.

Transfer the purée to a sieve set over a bowl. With a rubber scraper, force the purée through the sieve into the bowl; discard any tough peels or seeds that remain. *(The purée can be covered and refrigerated for up to 3 days or frozen for up to 2 months.)*

# Red Chile Pod Sauce

MAKES ABOUT 4 CUPS

**S**ERVE THIS LUSCIOUS RED CHILE-FIRED GRAVY OVER ENCHI-LADAS, BURRITOS, CHIMICHANGAS, chilaquiles, huevos rancheros, and on and on and on.

3 tablespoons olive oil

½ cup minced yellow onions

3 garlic cloves, peeled and minced

1 teaspoon ground cumin, preferably from toasted seeds (page 13)

½ teaspoon dried oregano, crumbled

½ teaspoon dried marjoram, crumbled

2 tablespoons unbleached all-purpose flour

About 4 cups (2 recipes) Red Chile Purée (page 57)

1 ¾ cups lightly salted chicken broth

1 ½ teaspoons salt

1 ½ teaspoons cider vinegar

¾ teaspoon packed light brown sugar

In a medium saucepan over low heat, warm the olive oil. Add the onions, garlic, cumin, oregano, and marjoram and cook, uncovered, stirring once or twice, for 5 minutes. Whisk in the flour and cook, stirring and mashing the flour mixture, for 2 minutes. Whisk in the chile purée, chicken broth, salt, cider vinegar, and brown sugar. Bring to a simmer, then lower the heat and cook, partially covered, stirring often, until the sauce has thickened to a medium consistency, about 20 minutes. *(The sauce can be cooled completely, covered tightly, and refrigerated for up to 3 days or frozen for up to 2 months. Bring to room temperature before using.)*

# Pork Deshebrada
# (Shredded Braised Pork)

MAKES ABOUT 8 CUPS

USE THIS IN TACOS, BURRITOS, CHIMICHANGAS, OR TORTILLA CASSEROLES. Leftovers freeze well and can provide the basis for a tortilla-wrapped meal on very short notice.

1 bone-in pork shoulder roast
   (5 to 6 pounds)
1 large onion, peeled and sliced
3 garlic cloves, peeled and chopped
2 teaspoons dried oregano, crumbled

2 teaspoons ground cumin, preferably from
   toasted seeds (page 13)
2 teaspoons salt
1 cup Red Chile Purée (page 57) or
   frozen red chile purée, thawed (optional)
About 4 cups lightly salted chicken broth

Position a rack in the middle of the oven and preheat to 375°F.

Lay the pork shoulder fat side up in a heavy 6- to 8-quart flame-proof Dutch oven. Scatter the onion, garlic, oregano, cumin, and salt over the pork. Add the chile purée, if using, and the chicken broth. Add water to bring the level of liquid halfway up the roast.

Cover the Dutch oven, set it over medium heat, and bring to a simmer. Put the roast in the oven and bake, turning it at the estimated halfway point, until the meat is tender, about 4 hours.

Cool the pork to room temperature in the braising liquid. Transfer it to a cutting board, trim away any fat, and remove the bone. Using the tines of 2 forks, one held in each hand, shred the meat in a downward pulling motion. Strain and degrease the broth. (*The meat can be used immediately, or it can be moistened with the broth and refrigerated for up to 3 days or frozen for up to 2 months. Return to room temperature before using.*)

# Chicken Deshebrada
# (Shredded Braised Chicken)

**T**HIS EASY STOVE-TOP METHOD YIELDS MOIST SHREDDED CHICKEN TO USE AS THE FILLING in all sorts of tortilla dishes. It can also be made with turkey parts.

1 *large (5-pound) young chicken,*
  *quartered, including giblets*
  *(except the liver)*
2 *garlic cloves, peeled and chopped*

1 *teaspoon dried oregano, crumbled*
1 *teaspoon salt*
½ *teaspoon freshly ground black pepper*
2 *bay leaves*

In a wide 5-quart pan, arrange the chicken quarters in a single layer. Add cold water to cover by 1 inch (about 2 ½ cups) and set over medium heat. Add the giblets, garlic, oregano, salt, pepper, and bay leaves and bring to a simmer. Partially cover the pan, lower the heat, and cook, turning the chicken pieces once at the estimated halfway point, until the meat is very tender, about 25 minutes.

Remove the pan from the heat, set it on a rack, and cool the chicken to room temperature, uncovered, in the poaching liquid. Strain and degrease the broth. Skin the chicken, remove the meat from the bones, and shred it. *(The meat can be used immediately, or it can be moistened with the broth and refrigerated for up to 3 days or frozen for up to 2 months. Return to room temperature before using.)*

# Mail-Order Sources

**BUENO FOODS**
2001 4th Street S.W.
Albuquerque, NM 87102
(505) 243-2722
Fresh tortillas, fresh tortilla dough

**COYOTE CAFE GENERAL STORE**
132 West Water Street
Santa Fe, NM 87501
(800) 866-HOWL
Tortilla presses

**THE EL PASO CHILE COMPANY**
909 Texas Avenue
El Paso, TX 79901
(915) 544-3434
Southwestern ingredients, gifts,
autographed cookbooks

**JOSIE'S BEST**
P.O. Box 5525
Santa Fe, NM 87502
(505) 473-3437
Fresh blue and yellow corn tortillas, flour tortillas

**LÉONA'S DE CHIMAYO**
P.O. Box 579
Chimayo, NM 87522
(800) 4-LEONAS
Corn tortillas, wheat tortillas, flavored tortillas

# Index